Sound

by Emily Sohn and Diane Bair

NORWOOD HOUSE PRESS
Chicago, Illinois

Norwood House Press
Chicago, Illinois
For information regarding Norwood House Press, please visit our website at
www.norwoodhousepress.com or call 866-565-2900.

Contributors: Edward Rock, Project Content Consultant
Editor: Lauren Dupuis-Perez
Designer: Sara Radka
Fact Checker: Sam Rhodes

Photo Credits in this revised edition include: Getty Images, Cecilie_Arcurs, 29, Cultura RF, 11, iStockphoto, 4, Tetra images RF, cover, 1; Pixabay: Byunilho, background (paper texture), GDJ, background (tech pattern): Shutterstock: By natrot, 10, Everett Historical, 17, Nejron Photo, 27, SpeedKingz, 16

Library of Congress Cataloging-in-Publication Data
Names: Sohn, Emily, author. | Bair, Diane, author. | Sohn, Emily. iScience.
Title: Sound / by Emily Sohn and Diane Bair.
Description: [2019 edition]. | Chicago, Illinois : Norwood House Press, [2019] | Series: iScience
    | Audience: Ages 8-10. | Includes bibliographical references and index.
Identifiers: LCCN 2018057946 | ISBN 9781684509577 (hardcover) |
    ISBN 9781684043842 (pbk.) | ISBN 9781684043958 (ebook)
Classification: LCC QC225.5 .S645 2019 | DDC 534—dc23
LC record available at https://lccn.loc.gov/2018057946

Hardcover ISBN: 978-1-68450-957-7
Paperback ISBN: 978-1-68404-384-2

Contents

Note to Caregivers:
In this updated and revised iScience series, each book poses many questions to the reader. Some are open ended and ask what the reader thinks. Discuss these questions with your child and guide him or her in thinking through the possible answers and outcomes. There are also questions posed which have a specific answer. Encourage your child to read through the text to determine the correct answer. Most importantly, throughout the book, encourage answers using critical thinking skills and imagination. In the back of the book you will find answers to these questions, along with additional resources to help support you as you share the book with your child.

Words that are **bolded** are defined in the glossary in the back of the book.

Strike Up the Band!

Shhh. Listen. If you are out in public, you might hear people talking. Birds could be chirping. Sirens might be blaring. Our world is full of all kinds of sounds. In this book, you will learn about the sounds that surround us. You'll read about what makes sound and how sound travels. Along the way, you'll discover why sounds can be loud, soft, high, or low. You will also solve a problem. You need to design musical instruments out of everyday things. The concert is coming up soon. And the audience will be waiting!

How Can You Make Music?

Your school is throwing a big party. There is supposed to be a concert. Everyone has been looking forward to it for weeks. The concert is in a few days and you and your friends are the musicians. All you have to do is design a set of musical instruments. Then, you and your friends can play in a band!

You gather all the objects you can find. These will be your supplies for making instruments. Here is what you have to work with:

Materials

- plastic soft drink bottles
- plastic containers with lids
- dried beans
- rubber bands
- metal spoons
- cardboard boxes
- plastic rulers
- paper towel tubes
- toilet paper tubes
- metal cooking pot
- straws
- construction paper
- tape
- scissors
- water

As you read this book, you will learn about sound. Use what you learn to turn these objects into instruments. Your instruments should be similar to real ones, such as drums, guitars, flutes, horns, and more. You'll want some instruments to make high sounds. Some should make low sounds. Some should be loud. Others should be soft. Some should be able to make lots of different sounds.

If you put beans into a container and shake them, you can make sounds.

How will you use the objects to make sounds? Will you hit them? Blow into them? What will you do with the water? Read on. You are on your way to making beautiful music!

How Do Objects Make Sounds?

If you're like most kids, you make a lot of sounds. (Some adults might call it noise.) See how many ways you can make sounds with your body. Use your voice. Clap your hands. Stomp your feet. Listen to your stomach grumble. Write down all the ways your body makes noise. Can you play a song with just your body? How can you use your pen or pencil to make even more sounds? What else can you use to make sounds?

These boys are making noise!

When fingers pluck the strings, the strings vibrate. You hear the **vibrations** as sounds.

What Causes Sound?

All sounds begin with vibrations. When something vibrates, it moves back and forth quickly. **Pluck** a rubber band or a guitar string. Boing! You will see the object bounce back and forth. You will also hear a sound. Cell phones and many toys vibrate. Can you think of other vibrating objects?

You can't always see vibrations. Hold your fingers against your throat. Now, talk. Better yet, sing. Did you feel anything? Muscles inside your throat vibrate so you can make sounds.

Now you know that sounds come from vibrations. And you know that your ears hear those sounds. For all that to happen, sounds have to get from the source to your ears. Sound travels in the form of vibrations called waves. You can't see these waves. But you can imagine how they act. Drop a dried bean in a cup or bucket of water. Watch as ripples spread out from the splash. **Sound waves** spread out from their source in the same way that the ripples spread out from the bean.

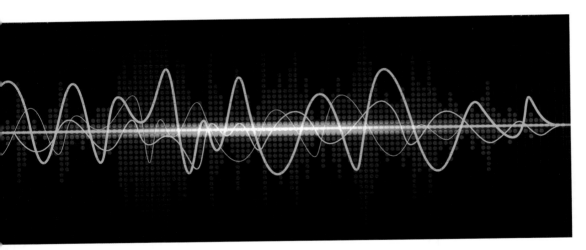

When objects vibrate, they create sound waves that travel to your ears.

Look at your iScience Puzzle list. Can you make any of the objects vibrate? Can you use two objects together to make vibrations?

Something in the Air

Suppose you could look deep into a sound wave. You would see lots of jiggling. Air is full of tiny particles. These are called **molecules.** When an object vibrates, nearby air molecules bang together. They're like a room full of kids having a dance party.

Sound waves travel from the air right into your ears. Small parts inside your ears vibrate. That tells your brain you are hearing something.

Sound waves make the molecules in air bump into each other, just as you would bump into your friends if you were all having a dance party!

Look at your iScience Puzzle objects. How can you use the objects to create vibrations? Which objects vibrate easily? Which objects do not vibrate easily?

Why Are Sounds High and Low?

Sing your favorite song. Notice how some **notes** are high and some are low. How high or low a sound is, is called its **pitch.** You can use your rubber bands to play with pitch. Put thick bands and thin ones around a box. Then, pluck them one at a time. What do you hear? Pull each band until it's stretched tight. Then try again.

Thinner and tightly stretched rubber bands should make sounds with higher pitches. That's because they vibrate faster. Thicker and loosely stretched rubber bands should make sounds with lower pitches. That's because they vibrate more slowly.

How can you change the vibration of your rubber bands to make sounds with different pitches? Try it!

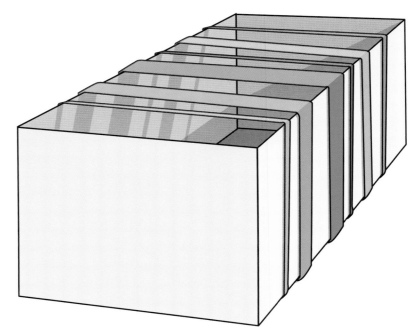

A fast vibration means that something bounces back and forth quickly. In turn, the sound waves jiggle the air molecules faster. You get more waves in the same amount of air space, thus the sound has a higher pitch. Remember back to when you talked or sang with your fingers on your throat. You felt vibrations. When you talk or sing, muscles in your throat vibrate. These muscles are folds of flesh called **vocal cords.**

Think about the rubber bands. Why do you think some people have voices with higher pitches than others?

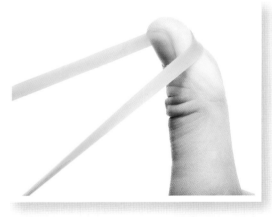

What can a stretched rubber band tell you about people with high-pitched voices?

Playing with Pitch

Put water into three identical empty plastic bottles. Put one inch of water into the first bottle. Put two inches of water into the second. And put three inches into the third. Which bottle do you think will make the highest pitch? Now, with one bottle at a time, rest your bottom lip against the open bottle top. Then, blow air across the top. What do you hear?

When making instruments out of bottles, be sure to use identical bottles. By adjusting the amount of water in each, you can play consecutive musical notes.

Your breath flows into the bottle and makes the air vibrate. The more water in a bottle, the shorter the air column. The shorter the air column, the faster the air vibrates. Which bottle makes a sound with the highest pitch? Which makes a sound with the lowest pitch?

A flute is a **wind instrument** that is shaped like a tube. It produces sound when you blow into it. A flute works like your water bottle instruments. But instead of adding water or taking away water to change the pitch, you cover or uncover holes. That makes the air travel a shorter or longer distance. The longer the air travels through the tube, the slower the air vibrates. In turn, the notes that come out are lower in pitch.

Grab an empty cardboard tube. Use scissors to cut a few holes in it. What else would you need to do to turn the tube into a flute?

How is your flute like this flute? How is it different?

When people sing together, their voices harmonize, or make music with different notes sung at the same time.

A Chorus of Voices

You can probably make your voice go high or low. Some people's voices go really high. Some go really low. When you sing, air moves across your vocal cords. That makes the cords vibrate. Faster vibrations create higher notes. Most women have shorter vocal cords than most men. So their vocal cords vibrate faster than men's vocal cords. That's why women tend to have higher voices. Your muscles control how tightly your vocal cords stretch and how fast they vibrate.

Can you think of a song that has a lot of high notes? Can you think of a song with lots of low notes? Which would be easier for you to sing? That might be a good song for you to play at the concert!

The Invention of the Phonograph

In 1877, Thomas Edison invented a device called the phonograph. He called his invention a "talking machine." It could record sound and play the recordings out loud. When someone spoke into the recording sound box, a stylus began to vibrate. The stylus cut small grooves into foil wrapped around a cylinder. Another stylus traced the grooves and made the sound play. The first recording was Edison reciting "Mary Had a Little Lamb." Later, inventors would use Edison's phonograph to create the record player. Today's record players use the same science as Edison's first phonograph. A tiny needle traces grooves in a vinyl record album as it turns. A cartridge attached to the needle creates electrical signals. These signals travel through wires to a speaker to play music.

When the phonograph was new, people would come from all over to hear it play music.

How Does Sound Travel?

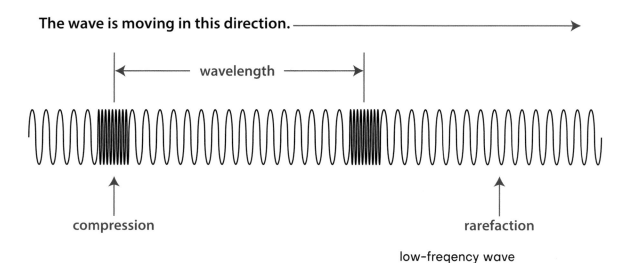

The wave is moving in this direction.

wavelength

compression

rarefaction

low-freqency wave

Water waves come in many forms. There are big ones and little ones. There are strong ones and weak ones. Sound waves are similar. Sound waves look like a spring toy when they travel. The area where the coils on the spring are close together is called a **compression.** The area where the coils are far apart is called a **rarefaction.** When a wave moves, the compressions and rarefactions move along the spring, but the spring itself doesn't move.

The wave is moving in this direction. ⟶

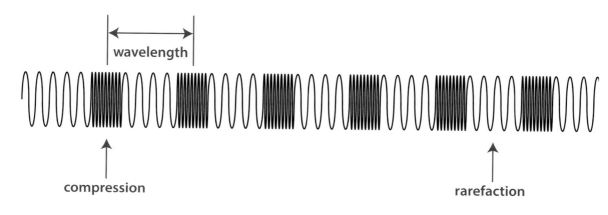

wavelength

compression

rarefaction

high-frequency wave

As the compressions and rarefactions move along the spring toy, or the wave, the wave's **energy** moves along as well.

A high-frequency wave has compressions and rarefactions that are close together. It produces high-pitched sounds. A low-frequency wave has compressions and rarefactions that are far apart. It produces low-pitched sounds.

Which items from the puzzle do you think would make low-frequency waves? Which do you think would make high-frequency waves?

Light travels faster than sound, so you can see what the drummer does before you can hear it.

Does Sound Travel Through Materials?

Sound moves through air. It moves through water. It can even go through walls. At sea level, sound travels through the air at about 1,116 feet (340 meters) per second. That's a distance of more than three football fields with every tiny tick of the clock!

Did You Know?

Imagine you're at a baseball game sitting far from home plate. You see the batter hit the ball, but you don't hear the crack of the bat until just a bit later. That's because light, which is what your eyes see when you watch the batter, travels faster than sound.

Sound travels much faster in water than in air.

When sound enters water, it picks up speed. Sound goes more than four times faster in water than in air. That means it travels about 13 football fields in one second! Molecules explain why. In water, molecules are packed tighter than they are packed in air. That means it is easier for them to bang into each other and move the wave along. Molecules are packed even tighter in some solids, so sound travels even faster through those.

Spy Games

Put your ear up to a door or a wall. You might be able to hear what's going on in the room next door. How much you hear depends on a few things. If there is a lot of space for air in the wall, a lot of sound will pass through to your ears. Thick or padded walls allow some sound waves to pass through but also **absorb** a lot of the sound waves. That makes sounds coming through those walls hard to hear. Also, when sound waves hit a solid surface, some of them **reflect,** or bounce back toward the source. That means some of the sound waves don't enter the wall at all.

You might be able to hear what's going on in the room next door if you listen very closely.

Sound bounces off the surfaces it hits, so in a room it bounces off the walls, ceiling, and floor.

Sound is a bit like a tennis ball. It can bounce from the wall to the floor to another wall, and so on. Sound waves bounce really well off metal surfaces. When sound bounces a lot, you might hear an echo, echo, echo…

Think about where you want to play your concert. Should the room be big or small? What should the walls be made of? Would you want to hang anything on the walls or cover the floor? How might you test your ideas?

What Makes Sounds Louder or Softer?

This is what musical notes look like.

You want everyone to hear the music you play. One way to make sure that happens is to put their chairs close to the band. Then if you blow into a bottle right next to the crowd, the sound will seem loud to the audience. You could also put the audience farther away and blow really hard. Pick a few objects from your iScience Puzzle list. Can they all make loud and soft sounds? Do some of them make loud sounds more easily than soft sounds? How many different notes can you play on your instruments? How loudly can you play? How softly can you play?

Going the Distance

Standing next to a rock band can hurt your ears. Back up a little, and the music starts to sound better. But back up really far and you won't hear the concert at all. Sound waves start out with lots of energy. As the waves travel, they lose energy. The farther they go, the softer they seem.

The sounds this young boy is making have a lot of energy!

Some sounds start out with more energy than others. Bang a straw against a metal object, such as a cooking pot. Now, do the same thing with a metal spoon. Which can you hear from farther away? What does that tell you about how much energy these two sounds have?

This Way, Please

When you dropped a dried bean into a cup of water, the water should have splashed and spread in every direction. We know that sound waves also travel in all directions at once. Do you think you can help direct the energy of some sounds you create? Send a friend across a field or playground. Try to yell something. Could your friend hear you?

Now, cup your hands around your mouth and yell the same thing. Your friend should hear you better this time. Your hands helped channel the sound in a certain direction.

At sports games, people use megaphones to send their cheers in one direction. That makes their cheers seem louder.

Look at the materials you have for the iScience Puzzle instruments. How can you use direction to send the sound of your instruments straight to your audience?

Using a megaphone sends cheers in a certain direction.

Audio/Sound Engineer

Sound engineers work with performers, musicians, and producers to create recordings. They make sure a recording has the sound the artist or producer is trying to achieve. Sound engineers combine different tracks into one recording. They might add a new instrument or a sound effect to a piece of music. They can make one instrument or voice louder than another.

Even though sound engineers may be in the recording studio with a musician, they complete their work later on computers.

Sound engineers also add music and sounds to movies and television shows. They use special equipment and software to mix music and soundtracks. Sound engineers help musicians and producers turn their work into works of art!

Solve the ⓘScience Puzzle

Five minutes until concert time! Are you ready? Copy this chart on a sheet of paper. In the first column, each item from the puzzle list is shown. Next, list the kind of real instrument that object acts like. In the third column, write what type of sound this object/instrument makes (high, low, or both). Lastly, explain how to play the instrument.

Item	Instrument	Sounds (high, low, or both)	How to Play It
plastic bottles			
plastic containers with lids			
dried beans			
rubber bands			
metal spoons			
cardboard boxes			
plastic rulers			
paper towel tubes			
toilet paper tubes			
plastic straws			
construction paper			
metal cooking pot			

Beyond the Puzzle

Congratulations! You put on a great show. The crowd loved it. They even begged for more. Look around you for more supplies. What other instruments can you make? Try to create an instrument that changes pitch. Make one that can play both loud and soft sounds. See if you can invent ones that you can blow, tap, or shake.

The concert may be over for today. But the world is full of music for you to discover!

Glossary

absorb: to take in and not let back out.

compression: the area where parts of a spring-type wave are close together.

energy: the ability to cause things to change or move.

molecules: particles of a substance or a material.

notes: musical sounds.

pitch: the highness or lowness of a sound.

pluck: quickly pull and release strings on an instrument.

rarefaction: the area where parts of a spring-type wave are far apart.

reflect: to bounce back.

sound waves: vibrations in air or water that can be heard as sound.

vibrations: the quick back-and-forth movements of particles.

vocal cords: the parts of the windpipe that vibrate to produce the sound of your voice.

wind instrument: a musical instrument that is played by blowing air into it.

Further Reading

Albertson, Margaret E. 2018. *Music: The Sound of Science.* Project: STEAM. Vero Beach, Fla.: Rourke Educational Media.

Gregory, Josh. 2019. *Sound.* A True Book. New York: Scholastic, Inc.

Rake, Jody Sullivan. 2019. *What Is Sound?* Science Basics. North Mankato, Minn.: Pebble.

Winterberg, Jenna. 2016. *Sound Waves and Communication.* Physical Science. Huntington Beach, Calif.: Teacher Created Materials.

Additional Notes

The page references below provide answers to questions asked throughout the book. Questions whose answers will vary are not addressed.

Page 13: They have thinner or shorter vocal cords.

Page 14: The bottle with the least air (the most water) makes the sound with the highest pitch. The bottle with the most air (the least water) makes the sound with the lowest pitch.

Page 15: You need to make a mouth hole in the flute. You also need to make a covering for one end of the flute. This turns your flute into a kind of bottle filled with air.

Page 25: The sound made with a metal spoon has more energy than the sound made with the straw.

Page 26: You can make sure the end of the instruments where the sound comes out is pointing toward the audience.

Index